LAMENTATIONS

LAMENTATIONS

An English Acrostic

COURAGE A. LOWRANCE

RESOURCE *Publications* · Eugene, Oregon

LAMENTATIONS
An English Acrostic

Copyright © 2024 Courage A. Lowrance. All rights reserved. Except for brief quotations in critical publications or reviews, no part of this book may be reproduced in any manner without prior written permission from the publisher. Write: Permissions, Wipf and Stock Publishers, 199 W. 8th Ave., Suite 3, Eugene, OR 97401.

Resource Publications
An Imprint of Wipf and Stock Publishers
199 W. 8th Ave., Suite 3
Eugene, OR 97401

www.wipfandstock.com

PAPERBACK ISBN: 978-1-6667-8523-4
HARDCOVER ISBN: 978-1-6667-8524-1
EBOOK ISBN: 978-1-6667-8525-8

VERSION NUMBER 010224

Scripture quotations marked (*ESV*) are from The ESV® Bible (The Holy Bible, English Standard Version®), © 2001 by Crossway, a publishing ministry of Good News Publishers. Used by permission. All right reserved.

Scripture quotations marked (*NRSV*) are from the New Revised Standard Version Bible®, copyright © 1989, by the Division of Christian Education of the National Council of the Churches of Christ in the U.S.A., and are used by permission. All right reserved.

Scripture quotations marked (*NJPS*) are from the New Jewish Publication Society Bible®, copyright © 2000 by the Jewish Publication Society. Used by permission. All rights reserved.

To Mom

CONTENTS

INTRODUCTION | ix

1 THE FIRST LAMENT | 1

2 THE SECOND LAMENT | 24

3 THE THIRD LAMENT | 42

4 THE FOURTH LAMENT | 58

5 THE FINAL LAMENT | 73

BIBLIOGRAPHY | 81

INTRODUCTION

HISTORY

IN THE YEAR CIRCA 589 BCE, Nebuchadnezzar II set siege to Jerusalem, almost a decade after a peace had been made between them when Judah had accepted vassal status in the Neo-Babylonian empire, and merely two decades after the final defeat of the Assyrians—dreaded masters of the ancient Near East—by the Babylonians and their allies. After the Babylonians had achieved their ascent, the consolidation of empire began. The kingdom of Judah, which lay near the King's Road, stood between Babylon and her rival, Egypt. In the tumult of events following the fall of Assyria, Judah was now unavoidably drawn into the battleground of great powers. Egypt had already pressured her prior to be a vassal state among others, standing between the Euphrates and the Nile. After that, the Babylonians had done the same, but Judah's patience with the Babylonian yoke would waver, and she would look back to Egypt as an ally against Babylon. So far, she had avoided the calamity of complete and total conquest. Now, she could no longer avoid that fate. Soon, Jerusalem was to become an example to the surrounding polities what wrath was reserved for a rebel city.

INTRODUCTION

Lamentations is a collection of five poems, which have been labeled as individual chapters in the Bible. Their common theme is the sack of Jerusalem in 587 BCE, after nearly two years of siege. The sack of a city was a grimly common enough event in the ancient world that the accompanying charnel was well-known. A kind of stock set of images and even a stock narrative had wormed its way into the minds of the ancient peoples of the Middle East. First, the enemy came, then they surrounded the city, trapping its people inside. To be left outside in the countryside was death or enslavement; to be inside the city was to be preserved for horror. If your kingdom or city state was not powerful enough to overcome the force that came against it, usually everything came down to this final drama. After the besiegement, the people would begin to run out of supplies. At some point, the disease might even begin to spread amongst the densely populated, a process that would pick up speed as more were infected, adding to the growing pile of bodies. Starvation was the worst way to die, particularly because that way to death usually passed through temptation to cannibalism. One of the images common to the ancient imagination (and the reality) was mothers eating their own children (presumably after they had died of some more natural cause but perhaps not). In such a circumstance, poetic hyperbole simply becomes a necessary descriptive tool. Then would come either the surrender or the breach of the city. And then the sack began. Warriors would kill indiscriminately, unleashing pent up anger—born of boredom and the suffering of camp life—upon the unfortunate inhabitants, while probably being under order to murder as well. Torture was likely a feature of this final desperate scene. Women, whether young or old, received the double mutilation of

INTRODUCTION

not only being slaughtered as remorselessly as the men but being raped and abused as well. Even so, some would be left alive at the end of all this, though none unscarred, whether in body or mind. These were for slaves and exiles.

Lamentations itself is often considered to have been written not only within living memory of the events it mourns but maybe within the first few years following the destruction. Traditionally, its authorship has been ascribed by both Jews and Christians to Jeremiah the prophet, who prophesied in Jerusalem even during its besiegement. And although this is usually considered unlikely by modern scholars, it may be best to read the text as if it were written by Jeremiah, as an imaginative exercise, that may or may not be taken seriously as fact. Surely, given the opinions on the time of its composition, the weeping prophet could have written it without chronological implausibility. If it's assumed he had no role in its composition, that then opens up the possibility of multiple poets having their hand in writing each of the laments. From the start, for the sake of simplicity, I am going to assume that one poet is the author of all five laments (which is certainly possible). Meanwhile, I will remain agnostic as to whether Jeremiah is that imagined single poet and so will not be directly referring to the prophet by name as the writer. Instead, he will be referred to as "the poet" or "the lamenter," along with a further varied nomenclature.[1]

---

1. It goes without saying, but the lamenter was almost without a doubt a male poet. It is not utterly beyond possibility that the poet, or one of the poets, was a woman, but it is beyond plausibility given the historical milieu in which the laments were written. The fact that it is often a feminine perspective that is taken up in the text doesn't quite change the likely reality; the same literary perspective is often taken in the prophetic literature, which itself is composed uncontroversially by a male cohort.

INTRODUCTION

It is not inaccurate, I think, to point out that Lamentations probably holds a more central role in the Jewish tradition than the Christian. One way to state this fact is to say that Lamentations is an important afterthought in the Christian canon but a peripheral necessity in the Jewish. Every year, on the ninth of the month of Av—or *tish'a b'av*—it is a general practice to read Lamentations in a service that not only commemorates the fall of Jerusalem to the Babylonians, but also to the Romans in 70 CE, and other such disasters as have befallen the Jewish people. There are some parts of the Christian tradition that most certainly do incorporate Lamentations within a liturgy, but the focus is obviously not the same, and I doubt that most Christians have ever considered the event of Jerusalem's fall as important to themselves. They would, no doubt, find it important within the narrative of scripture, if they were versed enough in it. But as for spiritual reflection and practice in their own lives, it is more likely that the events in the life of Christ would tend to capture their attention as more relevant. But the two destructions, the first by the Babylonians and then by the Romans, have an almost equal importance within the Jewish tradition as the exodus narrative itself, in terms of key events which define the covenantal chronology.[2]

THE POETIC INTERPRETATION

What follows is not an academic translation. I am neither an expert in Hebrew nor a scholar of ancient Israel.

---

2. Note the way that Josephus—in *Antiquities*, book 10, chapter 8—includes a chronology that extends from creation to the flood, to the exodus, to the building of Solomon's Temple, and finally to the destruction of that temple by the Babylonians, the loss of Jerusalem, and exile.

INTRODUCTION

That being said, I am a continually improving student of the Hebrew Bible, and in the course of working up this current poetic rendering, I did utilize the Masoretic Text (abbreviated *MT*) as my source, and the Septuagint (abbreviated *LXX*) as a supplement to it. Really, this began as a set of self-imposed exercises for working my way through translating some of the shorter books in the third portion of the Hebrew Bible, the Writings. It somehow began to make sense to combine my desire to practice writing poetry, so verse-exercises, with these language-learning endeavors. And so, verse by verse, it began to come together.

To add to this, only some months prior to starting what would become this project, I had read Robert Alter's *The Art of Biblical Poetry* and was absolutely enthralled by its contents.[3] Alter was both a muse and a locksmith for me. As a muse, the translations of Hebrew poetry found in his book felt so rich and new, even though the texts were technically already familiar to me. As a locksmith, his analysis of the dynamics of biblical poetry were nothing short of a light-year ahead of anything given to me in commentaries or textbooks up until that point, and I admit I gobbled it up eagerly.[4] If I had any awareness of the

---

3. Alter, *Art of Biblical Poetry*.

4. To note, biblical scholars are not often noted for their devotion to poetry and verse, ancient or otherwise, which explains some of this dearth. A comparison of Alter's translations of Hebrew poetry to most other English attempts should reveal to the reader, even one not familiar with the original language, the rather sharp difference. I further note that even so astute a literary critic as C. S. Lewis could only roughly parrot what passed as common knowledge about the forms of Hebrew poetry (*Reflections on the Psalms*, 3–7). To be fair, Lewis was unfamiliar with Hebrew. Yet the fact that a critic, with such a breadth of understanding in the poetic riches and versifying apparatus of multiple languages, ranging from the

INTRODUCTION

more detailed patterns of biblical poetry at all as I went about my little exercises, it was because of Alter.

The results of all this do not, thus, amount to a translation, something to be done by responsible scholars or committees of them: I can't adjudicate on the precise meanings of obscure Hebrew words or which textual variants to select over others. Instead, I think it's best to call this a "poetic interpretation" of the text of Lamentations. As such, I will be rather looser in my efforts than someone else may be. I take liberties that would be egregious to an academic translator and would raise the eyebrows of anyone concerned about the accuracies of what might be to them a sacred text. Nevertheless, admitting this upfront should stem some negative reaction to this fact, and I also add that I have never intentionally departed from what I think the spirit of the original might be, although I am not and cannot be a perfect judge on the matter.

Another way of describing this interpretation is to state that aesthetics, not exactness is the primary priority throughout. And I think there are ways in which, by pursuing unapologetically this end, the original can appear through the haze of time maybe in ways it would not otherwise. Select almost any English translation of Lamentations, and you will get what amounts to an accurate rendition. If you read Alter's version, you will probably

---

ancient to the modern world, could miss even just a few of the more intricate details of biblical verse does go to demonstrate this recurring pattern of ignorance. What makes this even more remarkable is that Lewis was rather familiar with the biblical text in English from before he was even a Christian, and after his conversion, it was read by him nearly daily for decades. What this must show then is the necessity to take part in a developed tradition of poetic criticism without which the individual critic might seem lost upriver without any paddles.

INTRODUCTION

get a better idea as to the literary style of the original.[5] But I couldn't find nearly any that tried to transform the Hebrew poetry into a text that sounded poetic in English or appreciated as much the ways in which the English language can achieve its own particular effects. That is not to say that Hebrew versification has no relationship with English poetics. Indeed, only a brief consideration of the way that the Authorized Version has affected the tone and style of English verse over the last few centuries, a translation that itself did allow Hebrew poetics to inform its own in certain respects, will reveal to the reader the fact that English verse has for some time already maintained a distant symbiotic relationship with Hebrew verse. If at all possible, I would like to have participated in that symbiosis in some small measure. And so, as I went along, I did carry this desire, a little flame, in my chest. Again, whether I can succeed isn't for me to determine, but I did enjoy the process of attempting it.

I kept a journal of sorts, in the form of notes and notions, as I went verse by verse through Lamentations, sometimes just a verse a day. These formed the basis of what are the notes within the text that follows. I included them at the end of each lament, so that they might form a series of endnotes for reference while working one's way through. They are meant merely to enhance the reading experience, as we each already enjoy an inner dialogue of sorts with what we are reading. By adding my voice to the reader's, a somewhat more multifaceted conversation can play out then. I hope that it encourages others to look in the text to see what they might be able to find and reflect on at their pleasure. I especially hoped to highlight these few areas: 1) where I departed in some deliberate way

5. Alter, *Hebrew Bible*, 641–69.

from the plain meaning of the text so that I could take the opportunity to discuss the original's meaning and intent relative to my own decision; 2) where some observation about the larger structure of each lament might help the reader orient each verse with the whole; 3) last, but probably most of all, when the poetic techniques of the original poet deserve to be explicated. On this last point, there is a nearly inexhaustible amount of things that could be observed about the techniques of the lamenter—and many others have said much of them—but I limited myself specifically to what I was able to note for myself for the first time. Surely these observations have already been attended to by careful readers over the millennia, but the few gems I could tease out deserve to be highlighted so that the lamenting poet can receive all the praise he is due and that the reader can delight all the more in the intricacies of the text, as well as go back into each poem and try and search out its secrets.

Of course, the only way to discuss the original poetry in the course of this interpretation was to include the Hebrew text by some means. And so I decided to embed the transliterated Hebrew along with the English interpretation.[6] This had not occurred to me at first, but as I attempted to find a way of incorporating the notes within the text, I realized that I would need a representation of the original for those notes to really make sense. Now, I realize that most readers will not be able to understand the Hebrew, which is no matter, since this really isn't

---

6. The system I followed is called Brill Simplified. I will provide a link here to an explanation for the system, but it shouldn't be necessary for the reader to need the reference, the transliteration itself is fairly straightforward. "Hebrew: A Simple Transliteration System," Brill.com, https://brill.com/fileasset/downloads_static/static_fonts_simplehebrewtransliteration.pdf.

INTRODUCTION

necessary for the notes to serve their purpose. The intention for their inclusion is actually less for semantic reasons and more for phonetic ones. The reader doesn't need to understand the text, so much as to be able to recognize its sound patterns, especially in the consonants. This is one reason why the Hebrew was transliterated rather than represented with Hebrew consonants and vowels, since those might not be legible to everyone, which would defeat the whole point of their presence. And, in truth, it's rather exciting to notice the phonetic patterns in the text, and to glimpse the ways that the poet has weaved together all his labor for the ear.

As a final note, I have decided to call the book of Lamentations from this point on not by the familiar name by which it is generally referred to in English but by the simpler "Laments." There is no basic difference semantically between the two words, and one is easier to write and say out loud. Replacing the four syllable "Lamentations" with the two syllable "Laments" makes even more sense once you consider both the Hebrew and Greek names for the book. In Hebrew, the name of Laments is *'eikha*, and in Greek it is *threni*. Both are themselves two syllable words, and ones that I am myself more fond of in terms of the sounds that make them up; they fall off the tongue so well, and I have been in love with both names from the first I heard them. We get our name for the book almost straight from the Latin *lamentationes*, which means precisely what we think it means in English: a mourning poem or song for the dead firstly, and also for those who survive the dead and continue to suffer The Latin is basically a close to direct translation of the Greek *threni*, but the Hebrew *'eikha* is not so related to those later names for the book. Following a common practice in the Hebrew Bible, the

INTRODUCTION

title is also the first word that occurs in the book. It is also the first word in the second and fourth laments as well.

POETIC TECHNIQUES

The Acrostic

There are a few techniques that the lamenter uses that should be pointed out at the start. The first is the use of the acrostic, or more technically, an abecedarius. That is, a poem in which each of its parts begin with a certain letter of the alphabet, in this case set in ascending order from the first letter of the Hebrew alphabet *aleph* until its last letter *taw*. The parts that make up the first four laments will be called "sets" here, which are each a collection of lines that starts with a word whose head consonant is the corresponding member of the Hebrew alphabet, depending upon where the set is located ordinally in the poem. Since the Hebrew alphabet has twenty-two letters, there are twenty-two sets in the first four laments, and then twenty-two individual lines in the final lament. The final lament abandons the acrostic form so that its twenty-two lines do not begin with an ascending order of consonants. More details on the nitty-gritty will show up at certain points in the notes.

Just why the lamenter should have written Laments in this acrostic form is a question generally asked by its interpreters. I don't really have an informed opinion on that point, but I will add that I think the important question perhaps lies not in why the poet chose the acrostic but rather in *how* the poet uses this form to communicate in the first four laments. If the function of the acrostic can be discovered or perceived somehow, then it might become clearer what the overall intent might have been. As should be noted, sometimes a poet only realizes the full potential and purpose of a form after he has used it for a time, so that the intention is developed into actuality only through the act of composition. It's a rare conjunction that manages to fit exactly the right form to the right poetic vision from the start. Usually, the reality falls somewhere in between clairvoyant creativity and mucking along. At this point, though, I can only repeat the trope I have heard before and seems true to me: that the lamenter hopes to usher in an ordered form to the suffering that Judah has endured, that the regular and consistent pathway trod through the letters of the Hebrew alphabet reinforce the totality of the significance of these events, and that this comprehensiveness is to be repeated ritually, since acrostics do tend to lend themselves to memory and repetition—they feel designed for meditation.

Finally, on the subject of the acrostic, I will make a crucially obvious point. In the following interpretation, as will become apparent at once to the reader, I have attempted, above all, to maintain the acrostic pattern that occurs in the Hebrew, but in English instead. The English alphabet has come to substitute for the Hebrew in this case, and I follow its order throughout. One practical problem that presented itself was that some English letters have something a lexical dearth surrounding them: "Q" is probably one of the worst offenders in this regard, along with "X" and "Z." Consequently, I never use those three letters. I am helped by the convenience that Hebrew only has twenty-two letters, whereas English has twenty-six in its alphabet. The removal of three letters from the English sequence still gave me twenty-three to work with. "A" through "T", with the exception of "Q," occurs in every

INTRODUCTION

case, from the first through the final lament. "U," "V," "W," and "Y" were always my final options near the end, and I could select three of them and ignore one. But even though I granted myself the luxury of skipping letters, I still follow them in sequence. The letters at the head of each set in the English interpretation are always appropriately placed relative to the positions of other letters in the order of the English alphabet.

Only one other published book that I know has attempted the like; that is David Slavitt's *The Book of Lamentations: A Meditation and Translation*.[7] After having begun working on the project, once I figured that I was really going to complete it, I started searching for who else had perhaps done the same. I presumed that many in their private studies had probably done likewise, but how many of these attempts had escaped into the outer world I was unaware of. Once purchased, I read Slavitt's book with great pleasure and enjoyed every bit of it, and the fact that he had succeeded at a complete acrostic did encourage me to finish my own project. What makes his poetic rendition stand out is that, as an active participant in Jewish culture and tradition, he has both a spiritual depth and an historical consciousness that enriches the contents of his version of Laments beyond anything I can imagine. The reader should give themselves the privilege of finding and reading his poetic translation as soon as they may.

Parallelism

The second technique is parallelism. Rather than try and give what is impossible, a comprehensive explanation of what parallelism is in Hebrew verse, I will refer the reader

7. Slavitt, The *Book of Lamentations*.

again to Alter's *The Art of Biblical Poetry*.[8] But I can give what I think is the most general fact that should be known at the start. The basic principle of parallelism at the heart of biblical poetry is the relationship between the parts that make up a *line*. The terminology I will use here will consider the line the interconnected set of parallel elements, each of which individually we will call *versets*. Thus, the relationship between versets within a line is the core, of biblical poetry. And sometimes it is true that this parallelism involves synonymity. A nearly perfect example of this occurs in Laments 4:11a: "The LORD vented all his fury/ Poured out His blazing wrath" (*NJPS*). But even in this case, and generally speaking, this relationship has more to do with pushing the meaning of the first verset forwards in some fashion within the second verset, rather than simply restating its meaning in differing words, which themselves can never achieve exact synonymity and are never intended to. Lastly, in Hebrew poetry, sometimes there are three rather than two versets to a line, but that principle doesn't generally hold in Laments. Nevertheless, in this interpretation, I decided to render many lines as *tri-parallel* as well as *bi-parallel*, these two terms representing the difference between lines with two versus three versets.

Alliteration

The third poetic strategy to consider is alliteration. I plan on addressing this fairly often in the notes, so I won't go into too much detail here. Suffice it to say that it is rather common in Laments and throughout Hebrew poetry in general. But it is especially used as a phonetic technique

---

8. Refer especially to chapters 1–3, 1–103.

in Laments because the emphasis on an alphabetical acrostic highlights the play of individual consonantal sounds. I will note here that in some cases the lamenter prefers to not necessarily highlight the sound of simply one consonant playing throughout a set multiple times within various lines; sometimes he prefers to set two such consonantal sounds with each other, both occurring often in some kind of alternating pattern that truly resonates with the reader's ear once they are reading the original Hebrew. I have sought to replicate these kinds of patterns sometimes, but the English text between these pages is far less rich in this consonantal interplay than the Hebrew, I must confess. But as the reader has the chance to glance over the transliterated sets, I hope they can come to appreciate the subtle nuances and aural beauty of this technique.

Rhyme and Meter

I will address the more controversial element here, I should think, first. There is something like rhyme that occurs in numerous places, sometimes rather overtly, in the Hebrew text of Laments. At some places in the notes, I will point out where this occurs, especially in the final lament. Admittedly, the rhyme that occurs is not like English rhyme much at all. It is used along with alliteration to make the poetry flow and hold together a certain kind of sonorous beauty as it is read or chanted. There are no exact formal rules, such as is generally the case with patterns of English rhyme. It will perhaps be helpful by analogy to compare Hebrew verse to English free-verse in this sense, although that is a very tenuous analogy. Certain phonetic effects occur within the Hebrew poetry which are consistently used, but not in an exact formal scheme, and free verse in English sometimes utilizes the poetic resources of its language where it wishes, rather than in more precise formalized patterns. Again, not an exact analogy, but maybe it will be helpful for some readers, especially those who have some familiarity with English poetry in the modern period.

As for meter, there certainly is a metrical pattern in Laments. In fact, this is probably one of the most regular features of the poetry in Laments, along with the acrostic itself. I will only provide the most basic overview of it. There are three accented syllables typically in the first verset of the line and two accented syllables typically in the second, and though there is a certain amount of variation here, it holds roughly true. The only way to really appreciate this aspect is to go to YouTube and to listen to fluent Hebrew speakers, often rabbinically or otherwise religiously trained, read Laments out loud. Do yourself the pleasure; it is well worth it. Probably the best detailed explanation of meter in Laments that I encountered is given by Yael Ziegler in *Lamentations: Faith in a Turbulent World*.[9] Her book is also likely one of the best sources to read on the larger scale structure of Laments and its various poetic techniques in general. In fact, the seemingly endless depths of Laments that I cannot provide a full explication of, for lack of skill and space, is exactly what Ziegler can begin to reveal for the patient reader.

9. Ziegler, *Lamentations*.

1

THE FIRST LAMENT

1. *Aleph/A*

'eikha
yash^eva vadad
  ha'ir rabbati 'am
hay^eta k^e'almana
  rabbati vaggoyim
sarati bamm^edinot
  hay^eta lamas

Ah!
How lonely sits the city
  once full of people.
She has become like a widow
  who once was great among the nations.
She who was a princess among the provinces
  has become a slave.

LAMENTATIONS

2. *Beth/B*

bakho *tivke ballayla*
  vᵉdimʻatah ʻal leḥeyah
ʼein-lah mᵉnaḥem
  mikkol-ʼohaveha
kol-reʻeha bagᵉdu vah
  hayu lah lᵉʼoyᵉvim

Bitterly she weeps in the night,
  her cheeks are drenched with tears -
    and there are none to comfort her.
All her lovers abandoned her;
  all her friends betrayed her;
    they have become her enemies.

3. *Gimel/C*

galᵉta *yᵉhuda meʻoni*
  umerov ʻavoda
hiʼ yashᵉva vaggoyim
  loʼ matzᵉʼa manoaḥ
kol-rodᵉfeha hissiguha
  bein hammᵉtzarim

Cast into exile is Judah
  with her misery
    and the burden of her slavery.
She settles among the foreigners
  but finds no rest -
    her pursuers overtake her in her agony.

THE FIRST LAMENT

4. *Daleth/D*

darkhei *tziyyon 'avelot*
 mibbᵉli ba'ei mo'ed
kol-shᵉ'areha shomemin
 kohaneha ne'enaḥim
bᵉtuloteha nugot
 vᵉhi' mar-lah

Down the way to Zion
 none come to the festivals -
 her roads mourn their barrenness.
All her gates are deserted;
 all her priests groan.
Her young daughters are abused,
 and she herself worst of all.

5. *He/E*

hayu *tzareha lᵉro'sh*
 'oyᵉveha shalu
ki-yhwh hogah
 'al rov-pᵉsha'eha
'olaleha halᵉkhu
 shᵉvi lifnei-tzar

Enemies have glutted her riches;
 they have crushed her head -
For the Lord has wounded her
 for her many violations.
Her children are taken,
 captured by the foe.

LAMENTATIONS

6. *Waw/F*

vayyetze' mn-vt-tziyyon
  kol-hadarah
hayu sareha k^{e}ayyalim
  lo'-matz^e'u mir'e
vayyel^{e}khu v^{e}lo'-khoaḥ
  lifnei rodef

Far has the majesty of Zion's Daughter fled -
  her princes are like deer who find no pasture:
though starved and weak,
  they flee their hunters.

7. *Zayin/G*

zakh^{e}ra *y^{e}rushalaim*
  y^{e}mei 'onyah um^{e}rudeha
kol maḥamudeha 'asher
  hayu mimei qedem
binfol 'ammah b^{e}yad-tzar
  v^e'ein 'ozer lah
ra'uha tzarim saḥaqu
  'al mishbatteha

Gone are the treasures of Jerusalem,
  her own from days of old.
She remembers them in the days of her affliction;
  in her exile she recalls them.
When her people fell into the enemy's hands,
  there were none to help her -
Her tormentors leered at her;
  they jeered her downfall.

THE FIRST LAMENT

8. *Heth/H*

*ḥet*ᵉ*' ḥat*ᵉ*a y*ᵉ*rushalaim*
  *'al-ken l*ᵉ*nida hayata*
*kol-m*ᵉ*khabb*ᵉ*deha hizziluha*
  ki-ra'u 'ervatah
gam-hi' ne'enḥa
  vattashov 'aḥor

Horrible is the sin of Jerusalem -
  so she has become revolting.
All who praised her now revile her,
  for they see her stripped naked.
She too wretches at herself
  and turns away in deep regret.

9. *Teth/I*

tum'atah *b*ᵉ*shuleha*
  *lo' zakh*ᵉ*ra 'aḥaritah*
*vattered p*ᵉ*la'im*
  *'ein m*ᵉ*naḥem lah*
*r*ᵉ*'e yhwh 'et-'onyi*
  ki higdil 'oyev

Into her skirts her blood soaks down.
  She has forgotten her hope.
She collapses to the ground in shock -
  Abandoned, and none console her.
"Lord! Look at my misery!
  The ravager has overcome me!"

LAMENTATIONS

10. *Yod/J*

yado paras tzar
  'al kol-maḥamaddeha
ki-ra'ata goyim
  ba'u miqdashah
'asher tzivvita lo'-yavo'u
  vaqqahal lakh

Jerusalem's beauties are pillaged,
  grasped in the besieger's hand.
So she has witnessed outsiders rape her sanctuary,
  those who were never to enter there!
    the place where your people gathered.

11. *Kaf/K*

kol-'ammah ne'enaḥim
  mᵉvaqqᵉshim leḥem
natᵉnu maḥamavdeyhem bᵉ'okhel
  lᵉhashiv nafesh
rᵉ'e yhwh vᵉhabbita
  ki hayiti zolela

Keen were her people for bread;
  they moaned with hunger.
They traded their valuables for food,
  anything to revive their strength.
"Look, O Lord, and see!
  I am utterly despised!

THE FIRST LAMENT

12. *Lamed/L*

lo' *'aleikhem kol-'ov^{e}rei derekh*
  habbitu ur^e'u
'im-yesh makh'ov k^{e}makh'ovi
  'asher 'olal li
'asher hoga yhwh
  b^{e}yom ḥaron 'appo

"**Linger** and see all you who pass by –
  Is it nothing to you?!
Is there any pain like my pain,
  the pangs inflicted upon me?
The Lord brought them upon me
  in the day when his anger fiercely burned.

13. *Mem/M*

mimmarom *shalaḥ-'esh*
  b^e'atzmotay vayyirdenna
paras reshet l^{e}raglay
  heshivani 'aḥor
n^{e}tanani shomema
  kol-hayyom dava

"**Myriad** rains of fire he poured down
  to soak my bones in flames.
He spread a net to trap my feet;
  he flipped me on my back.
He left me there;
  I grow weaker by the hour.

14. *Nun/N*

nisqad *'ol p^esha'ay*
  b^eyado yistar^egu
'alu 'al-tzavva'ri
  hikhshil koḥi
n^etanani 'adonay bidei
  lo'-'ukhal qum

"**Knotted** into a yoke are my transgressions;
  his hands twist them together.
They are pressed down upon my neck;
  I buckle under their weight.
So the Overseer has given me up
  into hands I cannot resist.

15. *Samek/O*

silla *khol-'abbiray*
  'adonay b^eqirbi
qara' 'alay mo'ed
  lishbor baḥuray
gat darakh 'adonay
  livtulat bat-y^ehuda

"**Out** of my midst the Commander cast my warriors -
  he summoned a horde against me
    to trample my young men.
The Master treads the winepress;
  he bleeds the Daughter of Judah.

THE FIRST LAMENT

16. *Ayin/P*

'al-'elle 'ani vokhiyya
  'eini 'eini yor^eda mayim
ki-raḥaq mimmenni m^enaḥem
  meshiv nafshi
hayu vanay shomemim
  ki gavar 'oyev

"**Pools** of water fill my eyes,
  and I weep, weep for all this woe!
So far from me is any comforter
  who could breathe back life in me.
Now my children are orphaned,
  for the enemy has finished his murder."

17. *Pe/R*

per^esa tziyyon b^eyadeha
  'ein m^enaḥem lah
tzivva yhwh l^eya'aqov
  s^evivayw tzarayw
hay^eta y^erushalaim
  l^enidda beineihem

Reaching out her hands Zion pled.
  She begged for someone to comfort her,
    but no one came for her.
The Lord has uttered this doom upon Jacob,
  that his enemies should besiege him.
Jerusalem became a cesspool,
  reeking in their midst.

18. *Tsade/S*

tzaddiq hu' yhwh
 ki fihu mariti
shim'u-na' khol-'mym
 ur^e'u makh'ovi
b^etulotay uvaḥuray
 hal^ekhu vashshevi

"**Surely** justified is the Lord
 for all he's brought upon me,
  for I have rebelled against his rule.
All people, hear this!
 Witness my suffering!
Look at my young!
 They are led away to captivity.

19. *Qof/T*

qara'ti lam'ahavay
 hemma rimmuni
kohanay uz^eqenay ba'ir gava'u
ki-viqshu 'okhel lamo
 v^eyashivu 'et-nafsham

"**To** my lovers all I called out,
 but they discarded me.
My priests and my elders -
 they perished in the city.
They searched for food to revive their strength,
 but nothing was found.

THE FIRST LAMENT

20. *Resh/U*

reʾe yhwh ki-tzar-li
  meʿay ḥomarmaru
nehpakh libbi beqirbi
  ki maro mariti
miḥutz shikkela-ḥerev
  babbayit kammavet

"**Under** great terror I am nauseous
  and my heart beats hard within.
Please, O Lord! See my panic!
  Though I have been so rebellious.
Out in the street the sword slaughters,
  and in the house haunts death.

21. *Sin, Shin/V*

shameʿu ki neʾenaḥa ʾani
  ʾein menaḥem li
kol-ʾoyevay shameʿu raʿati sasu
  ki ʾatta ʿasita
heveʾta yom-qaraʾta
  veyihyu khamoni

"**Vast** is my trouble that my enemies witness -
  they celebrate that you have brought it.
They heard me sobbing,
  but they cared not to comfort me.
You have mustered the day you summoned -
  Now do to them as you have done to me!

LAMENTATIONS

22. *Taw*/W

tavo' khol-ra'atam lᵉfanekha
 vᵉ'olel lamo
ka'asher 'olalta li
 'al kol-pᵉsha'ay
ki-rabbot 'anḥotay vᵉlibbi davvay

"**Waste** them with woe
 as you have wasted me!
Without remorse you judged all my crimes:
 now let all their evils come before you!
O my groans are many
 and my heart fails within me!"

NOTES

Following a common pattern pattern inthe Hebrew Bible, the first word that occurs in the book becomes its name: *'eikha*. It occurs in three other instances in Laments: 2:1; 4:1, 2b, which also means that it is the first word in second and fourth laments as well. It is often translated with the English "Alas," which, in relation to our present case, does have the virtue of beginning with the first letter of the English alphabet. The reason for the more guttural and emotional "Ah!" is twofold. First, I already mentioned in the introduction that I threw precision out for aesthetics; second, "alas" is more reflective and softer in its meaning now, almost an artificially dramatic or poetic formalism, and so is not as appropriate as something that has a more visceral quality. Since *'eikha* occurs four times in total in Laments, it thus occurs twice as often in its exclamatory sense than elsewhere in the Hebrew Bible, according to the *BDB*, 32.[1] Those two other instances are Isa 1:21 and Jer 48:17, which is not exactly an abundance of referential riches. But the *BDB* also records its occurrences as an interrogative, which I will give for the reader here briefly and comment: Deut 1:12; 7:17; 12:30; 18:21; 32:30; Judg 20:3; 2 Kgs 6:15; Jer 8:8; Ps 73:11. In its interrogative sense, ’eikha means "how?" in the sense of "in what manner?" But that is its general meaning, measured across its various usages as an interrogative. In most of the cases in which it occurs, there is the added nuance that there is some measure of disbelief, shock, or concern that by some means a thing has taken place or will take place. Psalm 73:11 is a good example of an expression of disbelief, "Then they say, 'How could God know?/Is there knowledge with the Most High?" (*NJPS*). Judges 20:3 is probably the best example of shock or surprised disbelief. These nuances don't hold true for every occurrence of ’eikha, but they relate most directly to the use of ’eikha as an exclamation, where the sense does appear to contain a similar emotional valence. That is something like this coldly put: "*How could it be* that *this* is how things have come to be?" But the actual emotional sense of it is harder to convey outside of just reading the laments themselves.

The basic mood of Laments is mournfulness, moving from reflective moments to vivid and violent scenes and images, creating a sweeping panorama of not only the destruction of Jerusalem but also of the internal destruction wrecked by witnessing the things mourned. The need I think to dwell on the meaning of the word ’eikha comes from the way in which the basic emotional, and ultimately

---

1. Brown et al., *Brown-Driver-Briggs Hebrew and English Lexicon*. Throughout abbreviated as *BDB*.

theological, perspective of Laments can be discovered in the sense of that one word.

Aleph-set

In this first set, we already see a number of phonetic/semantic parallels used by the poet. Roughly speaking, the parallels here are occurring not only within the lines, between the versets, but also between those lines in varying patterns. Note that the second versets of both lines 1 and 2 both contain the word *rabbati*—an adjective, "much; many, great" (*BDB*, 912). Then, the second verset of line 1 as well as the first verset of line 2 both begin with the consonant *he*, and vt. 6 at the end of the set does the same, meaning half the lines in *aleph-set* start with the same consonant. Add another parallel, vt. 4 begins with *rabbati* and vt. 5 begins with *sarati*. The first two consonants in both vary from the other, but the final consonants match, and all the vowels in the two words match as well. In other words, they rhyme—and rather richly at that. It might be called a grammatical/phonetic coincidence if it weren't for the fact that *sarati* means "princess," a female noble figure—the patriarch Abraham's wife, *Sarah*, is named with the same noun (*BDB*, 979). Given that Lady Zion is called "great among the nations" in vt. 4, and that this parallels her being called "a princess among the provinces" in the immediately following verset, the two words are set up as semantically parallel as well as phonetically so. The proximity of the two words, combined with these two kinds of parallelism, are exactly the kind of evidence we need to see and take note of a legitimate and not accidental pattern.

THE FIRST LAMENT

Beth-set

Throughout the Laments, almost without fail, the lines occur within the sets in precise patterns of six versets in Laments 1 (except for *zayin-set*), 2 (except for *qof-set*), and 3; four versets in the fourth lament; then, two versets throughout the final lament, but these aren't technically sets, just a string of twenty-two lines, each with two versets. The effect of this pattern is perhaps a sense that the poet is trailing off rather than reaching a crescendo as he ends his work(if there is a climactic poem in Laments, it would be the third). One other more immediate effect of this structure is that most—arguably all—of the parallelistic relations that occur within lines are bi-parallel rather than tri-parallel (in other words, there isn't a third verset to make a tri-parallel of related versets). This regularity is, like the acrostic, an antidote to the chaos and horror inherent in the poet's thematic material. Its form is set in contrast to the Prophets, in which the poetry can often relish in swinging wide for varying ways of expressing either doom or hope, and generally prior to the realization of either in time and space. Those prophetic poets look ahead to warn about the chaos and the drama of the future by representing it in terms of a powerful rhetoric, given appropriate expression in their verse-form. The Laments, in looking back at the destruction that befell Judah and Jerusalem, has no need to represent that chaos to warn about it; it already came. Now, its task is to pick up the pieces, if possible, and then arrange them in something like a recognizable order.

Nevertheless, while these structural points are true for the original text, I have decided for my own aesthetic reasons (which sometimes amount to a whim), to sometimes introduce tri-parallels where there were originally bi-parallels. It won't usually be an indication of what the original structure's composition was. Any reference back to a scholarly translation will serve as a quick fix for the reader who wonders at these wandering lines.

Daleth-set

Though I chose for artistic reasons in verse 4 to end with "and she herself worst of all," a better way to render it might be "and it is bitter for her," or "and for her it is bitter." That is the more accurate rendering at least: that the fate of the young women in her care is "bitter" for her to witness and to bear. The point in this versionhere is that it does manage to introduce the motif of rape early in the poems. It is a recurring motif, a harsh but poetically and historically necessary one. To compare the sack of Jerusalem to the rape of a woman (as will be done) is a kind of nested metaphor. Woman were indeed raped when the city was sacked, so taking a sub-event within the larger event as a metaphor for that larger event has a powerful if disturbing resonance. In this case, it is hard to know which side of the metaphor is more informed by the other, partially because they are so intertwined.

He-set

I took license with verse 5 when I wrote "they have crushed her head." Better for accuracy would be "they have become the head" or "they have become victorious" or something like that. But I would lose the metaphor in the latter case, and the first case is somewhat too obscure to an English reader of poetry who has less familiarity with that ancient Near Eastern metaphor. A good parallel for this is the metaphor of the horn (like that on a ram or a bull), which often represents strength or power on the part of a nation or individual. If I render it as I did, "they have crushed her head," it keeps the image of the head, but instead uses it more literally—but still not entirely so ("she" is still an image for a city)—so that they crush her head, and then that image serves as a metaphor of victory for the enemy, and so in some sense comes around full circle to the original metaphor. This interpretation also fits well with the rendition of "Enemies have glutted her riches." "Glutting" and "crushing" are powerful words in English for not only destruction but the visceral sense of the destruction of a body, organismal destruction. As well, the second line of *he-set* that contains the image of the Lord wounding Zion himself fits well with the language of physical assault already present there.

Zayin-set

Note that certain consonants, and not always the one that marks the beginning of the acrostic, are chosen as a kind of phonetic motif that will play consistently throughout a set. In the case of *zayin-set* here, that consonant is *mem*. It occurs in every verset, except for vt. 6. One has to be careful to set up a criteria of sorts about what patterns might actually form these consonantal set-motifs—there's always a risk of reading an intentional pattern where there isn't one, or of not noticing that a consonant is repeated no less often than any other in the set. Here are a few criteria to note while glancing through the transliterated Hebrew: 1) does the consonant occur in every verset (an exception of one verset is generally fine); 2) does it occur more than once in at least one, but better two versets; 3) does its occurrence outweigh the number of occurrences of other individual consonants in the set (always leave open the possibility that two consonantal sounds are being intentionally played off each other); 4) do these consonants occur on the accented syllables in the versets most of the time but with allowable exceptions. I will provide a few other examples here for the reader to check throughout Laments: 1:8 (*heth-set/heth*); 2:10 (*yod-set/resh*), 13 (*mem-set/mem*); 3:10–12 (*daleth-set/resh*), 22–24 (*heth-set/heth*); 4:8 (*heth-set/tsade*), 14 (*nun-set/beth*), 15 (*samek-set/resh*),). This list is not exhaustive of all such cases in which a consonant dominates throughout a set, but it is a helpful one. I will also note that sometimes this consonantal play only occurs in single lines or even single versets, but here I have been concerned only about when it plays throughout a set as a whole, and the purpose of this small analysis is to avoid confusing alliteration in versets and lines with alliteration that is occurring intentionally across an entire set. The examples of the wider uses of consonantal play would require an analysis of almost every line and verset, so I will only point out these features here to the reader so they can notice this for themselves as they forge ahead.

In Old English, there was an alliterative verse that used strict rules around this kind of pattern (such as the epic *Beowulf* was written in), where alliteration of a particular consonant or a vowel sound would occur within each line. No such strictness is maintained here in the Hebrew, but there is a consistent love of alliteration in Laments, which does reflect a remarkably consistent attachment to alliteration as a strategy for versification.

The phrase *yᵉmei 'onyah umᵉrudeha*, which is rendered here straightforwardly "in the days of her affliction;/

in her exile . . .," is meant to parallel *mimei qedem*, "from the days of old." The latter phrase refers to something like a golden age, in the deep past, a residual recollection of Solomon's time, when the temple was built that was destroyed by the Babylonians after the siege. The former phrase refers to the poet's present, which is harsh and indigent. Also, no doubt, the treasures that are referred to in this set are those of the ruined temple. First Kings 5–8 provides a wondrous description of the imaginal character of Solomon's Temple as it is constructed and then dedicated.

Kaf-set

Here we have the introduction of Lady Zion's voice into what has so far been a third-person perspective looking from the outside in upon her misery. The poet introduces the voice in the last line of *kaf-set*, tying it to *lamed-set*, as Zion's voice continues on through *taw-set*, with only *pe-set* reintroducing the third-person voice again. This means that Zion's voice comes in at the end of the eleventh set and continue on with the twelfth set. Since there are twenty-two sets in the poem, by virtue of the length of the Hebrew alphabet, that makes this the half-way point in the poem, so that half the poem is written from the third-person perspective of the poet looking on Jerusalem and half from that of Lady Zion, the personification of the city. Thus, we get both a third-person and a first-person perspective on these events. We also get the second-person as well, since Zion at numerous points addresses either her God or those who are looking at her from some other third-person perspective, so pleas given up to both mortals and God. This interweaving of perspectives is essential to the first lament's character, allowing for a potent set of juxtapositions on the events that have transpired against Judah.

Lamed-set

Notice how the final image in a prior set merges with the first line of the next set. *Lamed-set* ends with an image of the Lord's anger burning like a fire, and then *mem-set* begins with an image of fire pouring from heaven onto and into the Daughter of Zion, right into her bones (although the purpose of the image is somewhat different in this case, still compare to Jer 20:9). This poetic technique is something like that used in weaving or welding, or any kind of craft that binds physical things together, but it is here utilized, by analogy, with words. Let's invent a term, *set-weaving*, as a way of describing what the lamenter will do throughout these poems, binding together sets with similar images and themes. I note this technique here on its first most obvious occurrence, but, as always, now the reader can look out for this pattern for themselves.

Samek-set

The *set-weaving* technique that occurs between sets mentioned above is also used in a similar way to tie lines together within sets in sometimes rather imaginative ways. In *samek-set* there is an image of a horde stomping and smashing the young warriors of Jerusalem. Following this image in the next line, the poet gives another, of God himself, like a vineyard owner, treading his own grapes in a winepress. The redness of this process has always suggested bloodletting, and it intensifies with its color the former image. The effect is that we first have a rather literal image of people being trampled underfoot by a mass of violent men, and then we are given a more metaphorical image of grapes being crushed and spurting red juices. The merging of the two images gives us the blood that maybe escaped our notice when reading the first, more literal image. Now to us the battlefield is not just men being crushed and dying; now we see the blood gushing as it would upon the field as well as upon the winepress. The more literal image is of course the one that is enhanced, since the metaphorical image is less informed by the literal one. To compare a winepress to a battle might be a curious fancy, but to compare a battlefield to a winepress brings the sensual force of the violence to bear. For the original listeners to these laments, agricultural imagery would be more familiar than scenes of battle. Refer to Homer in the *Iliad*, constantly describing battle in terms of scenes that come from the farm, familiar to those who raise animals and crops.

Ayin-set

This line is often frustratingly rendered (there are exceptions to this, Robert Alter's translation of Laments being one of them, 650). All the English versions I have listed as my primary referents don't get across the semantic/phonetic moment. I will give my own straightforward version of it: "For such things I weep - /my eye, my eye, flows with water," and perhaps a better version of the last verset would be "my eyes, my eyes flow with tears," or something of the like. *'Eini 'eini*, in a literal transliteration, is just the repetition of "my eye." This doubling of words in Hebrew is a technique used in various senses, usually to express some notion of plurality or qualitative intensity or purity. A primary treatment of it can be found in *GHG*, sec. 123.[2] The repetition in this case could mean something like what is described in that section under (*d.i.*), namely that the sense could be "both my eyes flow with tears," but that's probably not what it means, and it would be dim poetry put as such in English. And remember, the phonetic aspect of language is important above all in poetry. The expression, in terms of the aural effect, of "my eyes, my eyes" lends the line a poignancy and a sorrow it wouldn't have otherwise, regardless of exact semantic meanings. Indeed, it's possible in this case that the primary purpose of the repetition is not grammatical but sensual, not that the grammatical sense isn't still present. Sometimes poetry takes advantage of grammar to achieve its effects, makes grammar its servant, so to say.

In this case, I decided to go with doubling the verb *vokhiyya* ("weep") rather than the noun *'eini* ("my eye"). If not common in English prose or conversation, it is common enough in English poetry or heightened rhetoric to repeat words in this way (the technique is called *epizeuxis*). It is the only example in Laments of this doubling, and it wouldn't have done to let it pass without representation in the interpreted poetic text.

Pe-set

The term *lᵉnidda* is a modified form of *nidda*, the basic meaning of which is "impurity" or an "impure thing." Refer to *BDB*, 622. Often used to refer to things that are ritually impure (particularly with reference to menstruation),

---

2. Wilhelm Gesenius, *Gesenius' Hebrew Grammar*. Throughout abbreviated as *GHG*.

it conveys, or can convey, an extra sense of disgust or revulsion, perhaps the desire to avoid or get away from a thing because it evokes instinctual discomfort. I have decided to go with the image of a cesspool to convey this in English, which not only contains the semantic content of the disgust reaction that would be concurrent with the original image, but also widens it to include a generic sense of human waste and excrement. Not to mention that this is actually an accurate image, since a besieged city would begin to pile up with garbage, waste, and bodies, and would indeed reek of death and putrification. It is unimaginable, not to the mind's eye so much as to mind's nose. Poetic meaning doesn't have to be pretty, just potent.

Qof-set

In verse 19, the last verset in the English interpretation, translated as "but nothing was found," is located in the *LXX* but not the *MT*. I preferred the way it linked up the versets in the arrangement, and so decided to import it.

2

THE SECOND LAMENT

1. **Aleph/A**
'eikha
ya'iv b^e'appo
  'adonay 'et-bat-tziyyon
hishlikh mishshamayim 'eretz
  tif'eret yisra'el
v^{e}lo'-zakhar hadom-raglayw
  b^{e}yom 'appo

Awful clouds of darkness cover the Daughter of Zion,
  the billowing rage of the Ruler!
From heaven to earth he has cast down
  the beauty of Israel.
He has forgotten his footstool
  in the day of his anger.

THE SECOND LAMENT

2. ***Beth*/B**

***billaʿ** 'adonay l' ḥamal*
 'et kol-nᵉ'ot yaʿaqov
haras bᵉ'evrato
 mivtzᵉrei vat-yᵉhuda
higgiaʿ la'aretz ḥillel
 mamlakha vᵉsareha

Brought down are the fortresses of Judah's Daughter;
 in his wrath he smashed them.
The Commander swallowed them without pity;
 not a single refuge was left over.
He has struck to the ground in shame
 her kingdom and her rulers.

3. ***Gimel*/C**

***gadaʿ** boḥori 'af*
 kol qeren yisra'el
heshiv 'aḥor yᵉmino
 mippᵉnei 'oyev
vayyivʿar bᵉyaʿaqov kᵉ'esh lehava
 'okhla saviv

Calamity he heaped on Israel;
 he cut off her strength.
He withdrew his aid
 within the enemy's sight.
He burned like a raging fire in Jacob's midst -
 he licked up all 'round.

LAMENTATIONS

4. *Daleth/D*

***darakh** qashto kᵉʾoyev*
  nitztzav yᵉmino
kᵉtzar vayyaharog
  kol maḥamaddei-ʿayin
bᵉʾohel bat-tziyyon
  shafakh kaʾesh ḥamato

Drawing back his right hand
  he pulls his bowstring
    and makes lethal aim like a foe.
He has slain all that are precious in our sight,
  who dwelt in the tabernacle of Zion's Daughter:
    he poured out his fury like flowing fire.

5. *He/E*

***haya** ʾadonay kᵉʾoyev*
  billaʿ yisraʾel
billaʿ kol-ʾarmᵉnoteha
  shiḥet mivtzarayw
vayyerev bᵉvat-yᵉhuda
  taʾaniyya vaʾaniyya

Engulfing Israel the Overlord swallowed her whole:
  He swallowed her defenses;
    he wrecked her strongholds.
He made loud in the midst of Judah's Daughter
  mourning and lamenting.

THE SECOND LAMENT

6. *Waw/F*

vayyaḥmos *kaggan sukko*
  shiḥet moʻado
shikkaḥ yhwh b^etziyyon
  moʻed v^eshabbat
vayyinʼatz b^ezaʻam-ʼappo
  melekh v^ekhohen

Famished are the feasting grounds -
  He has trampled out his sanctuary
    as a garden is laid waste.
In Zion the Lord has ended
  the memory of feast and sabbath.
In a lost temper he spurned
  priest and king.

7. *Zayin/G*

zanaḥ *ʼadonay mizb^eḥo*
  niʼer miqdasho
hisgir b^eyad-ʼoyev
  ḥomot ʼarm^enoteha
qol nat^enu b^eveit-yhwh
  k^eyom moʻed

Gone are the altar's sacrifices;
  the Majesty has abhorred his Holy Place.
He has delivered up her palace walls
  into the enemy's hand -
They raised a hue and cry in the House of the Lord,
  like once was done on a feasting day.

LAMENTATIONS

8. *Heth/H*

ḥashav yhwh lᵉhashḥit
  ḥomat bat-tziyyon
nata qav lo'-heshiv
  yado mibballeaʻ
vayyaʻavel-ḥel vᵉḥoma
  yaḥdav 'umlalu

How sure the Lord was when he destroyed
  the wall of the Daughter of Zion!
He made careful his siege-works;
  he withheld not his hand from destruction.
He made rampart and wall weep;
  together they grew weak and fell.

9. *Teth/I*

tavᵉʻu vaʼaretz shᵉʻareha
  'ibbad vᵉshibbar bᵉriḥeha
malkah vᵉsareha vaggoyim
  'ein tora
gam-nᵉviʼeha lo'-matzᵉʼu
  ḥazon me-yhwh

Into the ground her gates have sunk -
  he has bent and broken her bars.
Her king and her leaders -
  all are scattered among the foreigners.
Torah has ceased.
  Her prophets are blind -
    the Lord no longer sends them visions.

THE SECOND LAMENT

10. *Yod/J*

yesh^evu la'aretz yidd^emu
 ziqnei vat-tziyyon
he'elu 'afar 'al-ro'sham
 ḥag^eru saqqim
horidu la'aretz ro'shan
 b^etulot y^erushalaim

Jerusalem's elders sit sorrowfully in the dirt -
 they throw dust upon their heads;
  they clothe themselves in sackcloth.
Zion's maidens hang their heads;
 they grovel on the ground.

11. *Kaf/K*

kalu vadd^ema'ot 'einay
 ḥomarm^eru me'ay
nishpakh la'aretz k^evedi
 'al-shever bat-'ammi
be'atef 'olel v^eyoneq
 birḥovot qirya

Kept long with weeping I am weary,
 and my stomach is sick with shock.
I vomit upon the dirt for what I've seen -
 My People's Daughter ravaged,
  and her children collapsing in the city streets.

12. *Lamed/L*

l^e'immotam yo'm^eru
  'ayye dagan vayayin
b^ehit'att^efam kehalal
  birḥovot 'ir
b^ehishtappekh nafsham
  'el-ḥeiq 'immotam

Languishing, they said to their mothers,
  "Where is bread?" or "where is wine?"
while they fainted like a wounded man
  in the highways of the city -
while their blood spilled out,
  soaking their mothers' waist.

13. *Mem/M*

ma-'a'idekh ma 'adamme-lakh
  habbat y^erushalaim
ma 'ashve-lakh va'anaḥamekh
  b^etulat bat-tziyyon
ki-gadol kayyam shivrekh
  mi yirpa'-lakh

Much I would say of you,
  O Daughter of Jerusalem:
But to what could I compare you?
  To what could I liken you?
Would you be comforted,
  O Daughter of Zion?
For you are broken
  as by the roaring breakers of the sea -

THE SECOND LAMENT

Who now could heal you?

14. *Nun/N*

***n^evi'ayikh** ḥazu lakh*
 shave' v^etafel
v^elo'-gillu 'al-'avonekh
 l^ehashiv sevytkh
vayyeḥezu lakh mas'ot
 shav^e' umadduḥim

No truth did your prophets see;
 their visions were deceptive and vain.
They have not exposed your wickedness
 to return you from captivity.
Their oracles for you are lying words,
 misleading is their utterance.

15. *Samek/O*

***saf^equ** 'alayikh kappayim*
 kol-'ov^erei derekh
shar^equ vayyani'u ro'sham
 'al-bat y^erushalaim
hazo't ha'ir sheyyo'm^eru
 k^elilat yofi
  masos l^ekhol-ha'aretz

Onlookers pass by the way,
 they all clap hands at you.
They hiss and shake their heads
 at the Daughter of Jerusalem:
"Was this the city they named

'the perfect beauty,'
'the joy of all the Earth'?"

16. *Pe/P*

patzu *'alayikh pihem*
 kol-'oy^{e}vayikh
shar^{e}qu vayyaḥarqu-shen
 'am^{e}ru billa'^{e}nu
'akh ze hayyom sheqqivvinuhu
 matza'nu ra'inu

Pitiless are your enemies
 who gape at you,
  who hiss and gnash their teeth.
They cry, "We have devoured her!
 Ah! Surely this is the day we've craved!
  It's in our sights! it's in our grasp!

17. *Ayin/R*

'asa *yhwh 'asher zamam*
 bitztza' 'emrato
'asher tzivva mimei-qedem
 haras v^{e}lo' ḥamal
vay^{e}sammaḥ 'alayikh 'oyev
 herim qeren tzarayikh

Relentless is the Lord's pursuit
 to bring to pass what he pronounced:
The doom he commanded from days of old,
 to tear down remorselessly.
He makes the enemy exalt at your fate,

THE SECOND LAMENT

makes your foe mighty.

18. *Tsade/S*

tza'aq libbam 'el-'adonay
  ḥomat bat-tziyyon
horidi khannaḥal dim'a
  yomam valayla
'al-titteni fugat lakh
  'al-tiddom bat-'einekh

Swiftly the tears flowed day and night,
  like a stream they ran down
    as their hearts pled to the Master.
O Wall of Zion's Daughter,
  give yourself no rest,
    nor let your eyes quit weeping.

19. *Qof/T*

qumi ronni vlyl
  lero'sh 'ashmurot
shifkhi khammayim libbekh
  nokhaḥ penei 'adonay
se'i 'elayw kappayikh
  'al-nefesh 'olalayikh
ha'atufim bera'av
  bero'sh kol-ḥutzot

Tally the hours of the night
  from the first watch till dawn,
    tossing and turning with praying.
Pour your heart out like water

before the presence of the King.
Lift your hands to him
 for the sake of your children's lives -
Who are weak with hunger
 along every street and way.

20. **Resh/U**

***r*^e*'e** yhwh v^ehabbita*
 l^emi 'olalta koh
'im-to'khalna nashim piryam
 'olalei tippuḥim
'im-yehareg b^emiqdash 'adonay
 kohen v^enavi'

"**Utter** ruin is the fate you've meted to me -
 Look, O Lord! can you not see it?!
Should women devour the fruit of their womb,
 the children they bounced upon their knee?
Should priest and prophet be slain
 right in the midst of the sanctuary?

21. **Sin, Shin/V**

***shakh^evu** la'aretz ḥutzot*
 na'ar v^ezaqen
b^etulotay uvaḥuray
 naf^elu veḥarev
haragta b^eyom 'appekha
 tavaḥta lo' ḥamal^eta

"**Virgin** maids and unwed lads,
 alike with their elders,

were felled by the sword.
In the dust of the street they lay -
  you killed them in the day of your anger -
  you butchered and spared not.

22. *Taw/Y*

***tiqra'** kh²yom mo'ed*
 m²guray missaviv
v²lo' haya b²yom 'af-yhwh
 palit v²sarid
'asher-tippaḥti v²ribbiti
 'oy²vi khillam

"**You** summoned as to a festival
 all my terrors round.
On the day of the Lord's anger
 none who fled escaped
  nor did they survive.
Whom I birthed and nurtured
 my enemy has destroyed."

NOTES

Gimel-set

Kol qeren yisra'el means more literally "the whole horn of Israel." In biblical literature in general, the image of an animal's horn is a metaphor for the strength or might possessed by individuals or collectives. To cut or hew it off is used to indicate humiliation and defeat (read Jer 48:25 as a parallel example, among many; also cross-reference *BDB*, 901–2). I originally tried to preserve the ancient metaphor, but the real sense of the meaning always seemed to get lost, especially in the process of attempting to conserve the acrostic. Regrettable, given that these kinds of metaphors, however esoteric with regards to our own metaphorical arena, are the tangible stuff of poetics. If I had felt it fit with the rest of *gimel-set*, this would have been a possible rendering: "Cut to the root is Israel's horn,/hacked away by his wrath."

Teth-set

In a too rare instance of interpretative coincidence, the alliteration of *beth* present in the Hebrew—*'ibbad v^eshibbar b^eriḥeha*—is replicable in the English rendition, "he has bent and broken her bars." Even the alliteration of *resh* can carry through as a pleasant surprise.

The fourth verset is hard to carry over into English. *Tora*, in this case, does not refer immediately to the first five books of the Bible, but instead to something like instruction in the law of God, which would no doubt involve the material that we now call Torah. The *NRSV* renders it "guidance is no more," which I think is somewhat too vague. The *NJPS* gives "Instruction is no more," but that just goes to leave imprecise just what is being instructed. The sense here must be instruction in what God has commanded the covenant community of Israel to do—so Torah. It matters quite a bit that this is the case, since surely the whole point of the disaster that came on Judah, from the lamenter's perspective, was failure to live according to Torah. Now, following the destruction of the temple and the exile from the land, even the basis of instruction which could enable such a way of life has seemingly disappeared (note, answering this problem over the next millennium will give us rabbinic Judaism, a solution orientated towards the diaspora of Jews following both the Babylonian and then the Roman exiles). The prophets are referred to in the following versets as having also failed and so having ceased to function as prophets should, and this is likely a deliberate parallel with instruction in the law. It is nearly an incipient case of ordering scripture according to the pattern *tora* then *navim*. I couldn't figure out how to render this poetically without explaining too much, such as using a phrase like, "instruction in the law," or worse "covenantal teaching" or something odd like that. Transliterating the original word right over into the text seemed like the right poetic decision, in both a phonetic and semantic sense.

Mem-set

One of my favorite sets in the entirety of Laments. The image of the sea is used to great effect and is rather moving. In the Bible, the sea generally symbolizes destructive chaos, the closest present thing to the pre-cosmogonic state before creation. The more straightforward translation is "For your breaking is as great as the sea," or better, as the *ESV* so poetically manages, "For your ruin is as vast as the sea" (this might just be the most evocative verset in a most evocative set). I wanted to bring in a specific image that evokes just why the sea may have ever been associated with destructive chaos in the first place, and the sight of breakers at the seashore is certainly one of them. I will leave it to the reader to notice how the meaning has been shifted a bit, but I did still stick to the image of the power and vastness of the sea.

Ayin-set

The translation of *zamam* (refer to *BDB*, 273) as "doom" is somewhat dramatic, but I don't think it is too far off the mark, especially in a poetic context. More straightforwardly, it is translated often as "purpose" or "device." That is, not only something intended by someone, but the whole active process of seeking to bring it about. It carries a somewhat foreboding connotation with reference to God, inasmuch as the "purpose" being referred to is usually one of judgment. And "doom" carries a hefty weight in English and can poetically bear up the nuance of a fate unwished for. Also, note that this "doom," something pronounced in "days of old," is probably a reference to the blood-curdling threats in Deut 28. If it had been more recent pronouncements of prophetic warning that were the primary referent, then identifying these punishments as pronounced in "days of old" seems oddly placed. Previously, the phrase "days of old" appeared in *zayin-set* in the first lament, in which it seems to have referred to the time of Solomon and his father David, when the first temple was constructed. But though that time was nearer to the exile than the exodus and wilderness narratives, it was still roughly five centuries prior, enough temporal distance for the perception of it to fade into epic history and nostalgic memory.

Also, the order of the Hebrew letters *ayin* and *pe* are reversed here in the second lament. This isn't the case for any of the other three laments that also follow an acrostic pattern.

THE SECOND LAMENT

Resh-set

Just as in the first lament, here the voice of Lady Zion takes over, after having been exhorted in both *tsade-set* and *qof-set* to adjure the Lord. She responds seemingly to the poet's prodding and begins her final pronouncements and appeals, *resh-set* through *taw-set*, the last time her voice will occur in Laments. But even though it seems that this is the reprisal of Zion's voice from the first lament, the immediate metaphorical referent that is addressed in *tsade-set* is "the Wall of Zion's Daughter." I think the sense here is to emphasize the way in which Lady Zion is figured as the matriarchal protector of her people, Jerusalem's walls serving as the appropriate image in this case.

I will add that the images here might seem inconsistent to the reader. Zion (refer to *BDB*, 851) is the name used at times for the physical "mount" or rise on which Solomon's Temple was built (Ps 20:3 is probably a good example of this). It is often used as a synecdoche, whereby the city of Jerusalem is called by the name of its most sacred physical feature. Now sometimes Zion is spoken of metaphorically as a mother, often as deprived of her children or widowed. But at other points the phrase "the Daughter of Zion" or even "the Daughter of Jerusalem" will show up, and, as seems strange to the modern reader perhaps, to refer to the same referent herself (refer to *BDB*, 123, for an outline of this usage), so that we seem to have the image of a mother and of a daughter mixed. And although it might seem like a diced-up metaphorical space, it is necessary to accept that these different ways of referring to the same city are not exactly synonymous in the imagination and so narrowly avoid being simply inconsistent repetitions. The poet has received from the tradition of biblical poetry numerous metaphorical strategies for referring to the city of Jerusalem, the political and spiritual heart of the kingdom of Judah. The consistent through line is that these metaphors are feminine, so that the city is personified as a female figure, but in different ways as you traverse the text. Variety is necessary to keep the poetry engaging, and what one must appreciate is that most of these metaphors are not original to Laments or the lamenter; they are taken up and spread out in a carefully crafted fashion so as to not repeat some phrase too many times in a row. You will note that back in *samek-set*, Jerusalem is just called "the Daughter of Jerusalem," and the next time she is referred to is in *tsade-set*, where she is called "the Daughter of Zion." The poet would not have repeated the same phrase in a row, a strategy consistently utilized throughout the second lament. The proof for this is to look back even further, into *mem-set*. Note, Jerusalem is referred to twice by metaphor in that set, the first time as "the Daughter of Jerusalem" and the second as "the Daughter of Zion," which conforms exactly to the point made above. To make the case airtight, the reader should be referred back further to *aleph-set*, *beth-set*, *daleth-set*, *he-set*, *heth-set*, following which are the sets already discussed above. The pattern holds throughout all of them, and you will find the same to be true to some extent in the first lament, though this kind of usage doesn't really occur much at all in the other three laments.

Taw-set

For textual reasons, there is some trouble here. Translations either go for some variation of one of the following two options: 1) "You summoned, as on a festival,/My neighbors from roundabout (*NJPS*,); 2) "You summoned as if to a festival day/my terrors on every side" (*ESV*). The basic choice is whether or not one goes for "neighbors" or "terrors," or something of the like, in translation. For aesthetic reasons, not academic ones, I opted for the second.

3

THE THIRD LAMENT

1. *Aleph/A*

*'**ani** haggever ra'a 'oni*
  b^eshevet 'evrato
*'**oti** nahag vayyolakh*
  ḥoshekh v^elo'-'or
*'**akh** bi yashuv yahafokh*
  yado kol-hayyom

Affliction I have seen
  by the rod of his wrath,
as he took me and drove me out
  into darkness without the light.
Again to me he returns
  only to turn his hand against me.

THE THIRD LAMENT

2. *Beth/B*

billa vᵉsari vᵉʿori
  shibbar ʿatzmotay
bana ʿalay vayyaqqaf
  roʾsh utᵉlaʾa
bᵉmaḥashakkim hoshivani
  kᵉmetei ʿolam

Broken my bones,
  and gaunt my muscle and skin -
Besieged and surrounded
  with bitterness and woe -
Banished to dark places
  as the dead forever are.

3. *Gimel/C*

gadar baʿadi vᵉloʾ ʾetzeʾ
  hikhbid nᵉḥashᵉti
gam ki ʾezʿaq vaʾashavveaʿ
  satam tᵉfillati
gadar dᵉrakhay bᵉgazit
  nᵉtivotay ʿivva

Captured so I cannot escape -
  he forged for me heavy chains.
Crying out, calling for help -
  he shut out my prayer.
Carved stones he set in my way -
  he twisted up my path.

LAMENTATIONS

4. *Daleth/D*

dov 'orev hu' li
  'ryh bᵉmistarim
dᵉrakhay sorer vayᵉfashshᵉḥeni
  samani shomem
darakh qashto vayyatztziveni
  kammattara' laḥetz

Down in the thicket a lion crouches -
  there a bear waits for me -
Deadly is he that rips me off my path
  and tears me to pieces.
Dangled me for arrows,
  he bends his bow at me.

5. *He/E*

hevi' bᵉkhilyotay
  bᵉnei 'ashpato
hayiti sᵉḥoq lᵉkhol-'ammi
  nᵉginatam kol-hayyom
hisbi'ani vammᵉrorim
  hirvani la'ana

Entrails he has pierced
  with arrows from his quiver.
Entertainment I have become
  for a mob once my people
    who sing of me a mocking song.
Empty is the cup of gall and wormwood
  he forced down my throat.

THE THIRD LAMENT

6. *Waw/F*

vayyagres *beḥatzatz shinnay*
  hikhpishani ba'efer
vattiznaḥ *mishshalom nafshi*
  nashiti tova
va'omar *'avad nitzḥi*
  vᵉtoḥalti me-yhwh

Fallen into the ruin's ashes
  my teeth grind on gravel.
Far from peace my soul is cast
  where I forget my happiness.
"**Finally** my endurance is dead,"
  said I, "from the Lord no more my hope."

7. *Zayin/G*

*z*ᵉ***khar-**'onyi umᵉrudi*
  la'ana varo'sh
zakhor *tizkor vtseḥ*
  'alay nafshi
zo't *'ashiv 'el-libbi*
  'al-ken 'oḥil

Gall and wormwood!
  Misery and exile!
    Remember these I suffer!
Gathered are these memories
  into my very soul;
    thus, I'm bowed and weary.
Grasping for some better thing,
  I bring this hope within my heart:

8. *Heth*/H

ḥasdei yhwh ki lo'-tam^enu
 ki lo'-khalu raḥamayw
ḥadashim labb^eqarim
 rabba 'emunatekha
ḥelqi yhwh 'am^era nafshi
 'al-ken 'oḥil lo

How the enduring love of the Lord never ceases;
 how his mercies never end;
how new they are every morning come -
 great is your faithfulness!
"Hope I have in him," says my soul,
 "for the Lord is my portion."

9. *Teth*/I

tov yhwh l^eqovav
 l^enefesh tidr^eshennu
tov v^eyaḥil v^edumam
 litshu'at yhwh
tov laggever ki-yissa'
 'ol bin'urayw

Immensely the Lord favors
 those who wait for him,
  who seek him out.
It is good to hope,
 to wait quietly for the Lord's rescue.
It is good for a man
 to bear this yoke in youth.

THE THIRD LAMENT

10. *Yod/J*

yeshev *badad v*^{e}*yiddom*
  ki natal ʻalayw
yitten *beʻafar pihu*
  ʼulay yesh tiqva
yitten *l*^{e}*makkehu leḥi*
  yisbaʻ b^e*ḥerpa*

Just as his neck is forced
  to hold that heavy weight,
    so solitude and silence weigh.
Just let him eat the dust,
  maybe yet there's hope…
Just let him turn his cheek to the striker,
  let him eat his fill of reproach.

11. *Kaf/K*

ki *lo' yiznaḥ l*^{e}*ʻolam*
  ʼadonay
ki *ʼim-hoga v*^{e}*riḥam*
  k^e*rov ḥasadav*
ki *lo' ʻinna millibbo*
  vayyagge b^e*nei-'ish*

Kindness will not shun forever:
  for he who torments you
    is he who pities you,
keeping true his steady mercy,
  holding fast his affection.
Keenness for cruelty is not his heart,
  nor does he love humanity's pain.

12. *Lamed/L*

l^edakke' taḥat raglayw
  kol 'asirei 'aretz
l^ehattot mishpat-gaver
  neged p^enei 'elyon
l^e'avvet 'adam b^erivo
  'adonay lo' ra'a

Lo! Those who crush underfoot
  all the captives of the Earth,
long denying justice to youth
  in the court of the Highest,
luring a man into judicial hell -
  Dream not of the Ruler's approval.

13. *Mem/M*

mi ze 'amar vattehi
  'adonay lo' tzivva
mippi 'elyon lo' tetze'
  hara'ot v^ehattov
mah-yit'onen 'adam ḥay
  gever 'al-ḥt'v

Master, who spoke and it happened?
  Was it not you?
Most High, from your mouth
  come not fortune and ruin?
Man, while you live
  for what do you complain:
    would it be for your sins?

THE THIRD LAMENT

14. *Nun*/N

nahpᵉsa *dᵉrakheinu vᵉnahqora*
  vᵉnashuva 'ad-yhwh
nissa' *lᵉvavenu 'el-kappayim*
  'el-'el bashshamayim
nahnu *fasha'nu umarinu*
  'atta lo' salahᵉta

Now let us test our way
  and search out within -
    let us return to the Lord!
Now we lift our hearts upon our palms
  to the God in the heavens!
Never could we expect your mercy,
  after our crime,
    after our rebellion.

15. *Samek*/O

sakkota *va'af vattirdᵉfenu*
  haragta lo' hamalᵉta
sakkota *ve'anan lakh*
  me'avor tᵉfilla
sᵉhi uma'os tᵉsimenu
  bᵉqerev ha'ammim

O! you've wrapped anger about you
  and hunted us down -
    you killed without mercy.
Out from above you've come,
  concealed in a cloud -
    no prayer passes through it.

Old refuse and filth you've made us,
 revolting to all peoples.

16. *Pe/P*

patzu *'aleinu pihem*
 kol-'oyᵉveinu
paḥad *vafaḥat haya lanu*
 hashshe't vᵉhashshaver
palgei-mayim *terad 'eini*
 'al-shever bat-'ammi

Proudly our enemies laugh at us;
 they gape at our pain.
Pale with fear and trembling
 we are overcome
  with desolation and destruction.
Passing through my eyes
 the streams of water flow
  for the breaking of My People's Daughter.

17. *Ayin/R*

'eini *niggᵉra vᵉlo' tidme*
 me'ein hafugot
'ad-yashqif *vᵉyere'*
 yhwh mishshamayim
'eini *'olᵉla lᵉnafshi*
 mikkol bᵉnot 'iri

Rarely I rest from weeping,
 my eyes overflow without ceasing.
Return your gaze, O Lord,

THE THIRD LAMENT

from heaven on high -
  for then I will wait.
Wretched my eyes make me with weeping
  for the woe of all the daughters,
    the maidens of my city.

18. *Tsade/S*

tzod *tzaduni katztzippor*
  'oy^evay ḥinnam
tzam^etu *vabbor ḥayyay*
  vayyaddu-'even bi
tzafu-mayim *'al-ro'shi*
  'amarti nigzar^eti

Swift as a bird I flee my hunters,
  my enemies without cause.
Silenced in a dungeon,
  there they cast stones on me.
Surging waters swallow my head -
  I cry, "I am lost!"

19. *Qof/T*

qara'ti *shimkha yhwh*
  mibbor taḥtiyyot
qoli *shama'^eta 'al-ta'lem*
  'ozn^ekha l^eravḥati l^eshav'ati
qaravta *b^eyom 'eqra'ekka*
  'amarta 'al-tira'

To you, O Lord, I call
  from the deepest dungeon's depths.

LAMENTATIONS

Turn to my voice;
 shut not your ears
  to my need, my plea.
Today you came close,
 the very day I pled with you:
  you said, "Fear not."

   20. ***Resh*/U**

ravta *'adonay rivei nafshi*
 ga'alta ḥayyay
ra'ita *yhwh 'avvatati*
 shafᵉta mishpati
ra'ita *kol-niqmatam*
 kol-maḥshᵉvotam li

Utter, O Ruler, words on my behalf -
 plead my case,
  and redeem my life.
Undo the accusations I am tried with;
 see how falsely they charge:
  O Lord, try my case!
United against me are many
 who would revenge themselves,
  who plot endlessly.

   21. **Sin, Shin/V**

shama'ta *ḥerpatam yhwh*
 kol-maḥshᵉvotam 'alay
siftei *qamay vᵉhegyonam*
 'alay kol-hayyom
shivtam *vᵉqimatam habbita*

THE THIRD LAMENT

'ani manginatam

Venomous scorn you've heard, O Lord,
  all the intrigue to end me.
Violent lips my foes have,
  their thoughts all day churn against me.
Vicious are the mocking lyrics
  they sing of me ceaselessly.

   22. *Taw/Y*

tashiv lahem g^emul yhwh
  k^ema'ase y^edeihem
titten lahem m^eginnat-lev
  ta'alat^ekha lahem
tirdof b^e'af v^etashmidem
  mittaḥat sh^emei yhwh

You will pay them back, O Lord;
  return to them what their hands have done.
You will give deadened hearts to them,
  your curse will be upon them.
You will hunt them down in wrath
  and then wipe them out
    from under all of heaven, O Lord!

NOTES

It must be admitted that there are many and sometimes odd syntactic inversions in the following interpretation of the third lament. This is poetry and so it is more allowable, but still a word on it. Conserving the acrostic has necessitated this throughout. I take some comfort though in the fact that the Hebrew poet himself had to reckon with similar inversions in his own syntax and phrasing, so that each line could begin with the corresponding consonant in each set.[1] This is the central lament of the five poems, and also the most adamant display of the lamenter's commitment to his poetic form. Elsewhere in the biblical corpus, only Ps 119 attempts such an intensive form of the acrostic.

Aleph-set

This first set is a little narrative, a nightmarish inversion of the usual image of the shepherd caring for his sheep. The image of Israel's God as a shepherd, guiding the people as if they were sheep in need of a shepherd, is common enough in the Bible. And it is that very commonality that makes this twist wander into some uncanny valley on the metaphorical map.

Gimel-set

Gimel-set captures an oppressive sense of being locked in, entrapped by forces outside of one's control—worse still, captured by the very power that above all ought to be on the side of the lamenter. For this third lament is unlike the first or the second. In the first, the lamenter takes up the third person perspective, considering the suffering of Lady Zion, whose voice then takes over in the second half of the lament. The second, likewise, continues in the poet's voice until Lady Zion's voice takes over again and concludes the lament. But in the third, we get the lamenter's

---

1. Alter, *Lamentations*, 657. Refer to his commentary on 3:1.

perspective throughout the entirety of the poem, though he does not represent himself as an observer of Zion's suffering but rather asthe sufferer himself. In these early sets, a certain horrid trope is expressed in each, sometimes overlapping into each other—*aleph-set*, abandonment; *Beth-set*, the onset of death by wasting away; *gimel-set*, existential claustrophobia; *daleth-set*, being set upon by predators (human and beast); *he-set*, public humiliation. *waw-set* and *zayin-set* sum up this tension caused by the lamenter's suffering and lead to the climax of *heth-set*.

Heth-set

Waw-set through *heth-set* form a remarkable section. The rising tension of the poet's increasing despair reaches both its climax and catharsis in the oddly calm expression of trust found in *heth-set*, which may be one of the most well-known sets from within the entirety of Laments. The following three sets, *tcth set*—*kaf-set*, continue the theme begun in *heth-set*, outlining the real providential purpose revealed in the disasters that have afflicted the lamenter from the beginning of the third lament. Not only is the suffering instructive in intent, but it also cannot last forever, because, somehow, the ultimate purpose in the catastrophe of Judah's exile cannot be for ill but rather must be restorative. Instruction and restoration, each through suffering, then, are the two themes that are pulled up from the heart of the lamenter, right up until the mid-point of the third lament at the eleventh set, *kaf-set*. This was an ascent, from the darkness in the beginning, at *aleph-set*.

Lamed-set

What follows from the beginning of the second half of the third lament here is a kind of collective confession. The poet speaks on behalf of the community of Judah, admitting their sin to God, and also speaks to the community, pressing an acknowledgment of their wrongdoing. And so there is a consistent second person address that runs throughout this half of the third lament. The perspectival orientation of the lamenter is never merely inwards but extends outwards at the same time to God and the people of God, while not failing to also maintain the inner dimension.

At the formal level of analysis, the lamenter uses these shifting second-person addresses at one point to tie two sets together. At the end of *mem-set*, he shifts from addressing God to addressing an individual, probably set up as a representative of the whole community of Israel, an address that then becomes an inclusive second person (the poet is included among the "we" or "us" addressed) in *nun-set*, which is a confession of collective sin.

For the rest of the second half of this lament, generally the changes in perspective match to the beginnings of new sets. But in *ayin-set*, we have two lines of personal lament in the first person centered around an address to God in the middle line, as if the poet is gasping between sobs to say something in prayer.

Something similar to *mem-set* takes place in *tsade-set*, where the lamenter cries out a single word in panic, which might be taken as an address to God or just an exclamation, but it does transition seamlessly as prayer to *qof-set*.

THE THIRD LAMENT

Tsade-set – Qof-set

There is a small but I think poignant parallel that takes place in these two sets, not between versets or lines, but between the sets themselves. The final verset of *tsade-set* is *'amarti nigzar^eti*, and the final verset of *qof-set* is *'amarta 'al-tira'*. The parallel is formally in the usage of the verb *amar*, "to say, utter," which occurs in the first person in the former case and in the second person in the latter. The parallel is a contrast between the cry of the lamenter and the reassurance of his God, whose response is prompted by the previous panicked utterance.

4

THE FOURTH LAMENT

1. **Aleph/A**

'eikha
yu'am zahav yishne'
  hakketem hattov
*tishtappekh*e*na 'avnei-qodesh*
  *b*e*ro'sh kol-ḥutzot*

Alas! How darkened the gold has become,
  How changed from its purest form -
The holy gems are scattered about
  along every street and way.

2. **Beth/B**

*b*e*nei tziyyon hay*e*qarim*
  *ham*e*sulla'im bappaz*
*'eikha neḥsh*e*vu l*e*nivlei-ḥeres*
  *ma'ase y*e*dei yotzer*

THE FOURTH LAMENT

Bullion of gold cannot equal
  the worth of Zion's sons.
Oh! But they are regarded as jars of clay,
  the making of a potter's hands!

3. *Gimel/C*

gam-taniyn ḥal^{e}tzu shad
  heiniqu gureihen
bat-'ammi l^e'akhzar
  kaye 'eniym bammidbar

Consider even jackals give their breast,
  nursing their young.
But the Daughter of my People is cruel,
  like the ostrich in the wilderness,
    abandoning her offspring.

4. *Daleth/D*

davaq l^{e}shon yoneq
  'el-ḥikko batztzama'
'olalim sha'alu leḥem
  pores 'ein lahem

Dry the suckling infant's tongue
  cleaves to its palate,
and the children beg for food,
  but none give to them.

LAMENTATIONS

5. *He/E*

ha'okhᵉlim *lᵉma'adannim*
 nashammu baḥutzot
ha'emunim 'alei tola‛
 ḥibbᵉqu 'ashpattot

Eaters of delicacies are made to tremble
 out in the middle of the streets:
Enrobed in purple garments once,
 now they embrace refuse.

6. *Waw/F*

vayyigdal *'avon bat-'ammi*
 meḥatta't sᵉdom
hahafukha khᵉmo-raga‛
 vᵉlo'-ḥalu vah yadayim

Fire and brimstone consumed Sodom,
 but her crime was less
 than the sin of My People's Daughter.
She was overthrown in but a moment
 with no hand set against her.

7. *Zayin/G*

zakku *nᵉzireha mishsheleg*
 tzaḥu meḥalav
'adᵉmu 'etzem mippᵉninim
 sappir gizratam

THE FOURTH LAMENT

Gaze on her lords:
  they were brighter than snow,
    whiter than milk;
Their skin was redder than rubies;
  like cut sapphires their form.

8. *Heth/H*

ḥashakh mishsheḥor to'oram
  lo' nikkeru baḥutzot
tzafad 'oram 'al-'atzmam
  yavesh haya kha'etz

How now they are unrecognized
  by all who pass along the roads.
Their faces are darker than soot;
  their skin shrivels against their bones;
    as dry as wood their flesh.

9. *Teth/I*

tovim hayu ḥallei-ḥerev
  meḥallei ra'av
shehem yazuvu meduqqarim
  mittenuvot saday

If it were terror to die by the sword,
  worse still to die by famine.
They wasted away starving,
    for lack of the harvest.

10. *Yod/J*

y^edei nashim raḥamaniyyot
  bishsh^elu yaldeihen
hayu l^evarot lamo
  b^eshever bat-ʿammi

Joyful mothers with tender hands
  once held their babes;
    now those hands bake their children.
They became food for the siege,
  when the Daughter of My People was broken.

11. *Kaf/K*

killa *yhwh ʾet-ḥamato*
  shafakh ḥaron ʾappo
vayyatztzet-ʾesh b^etziyyon
  vatto'khal y^esodoteha

Kindling his fire in Zion,
  the Lord consumed her foundations:
He unleashed his fury;
  he poured out hot wrath.

12. *Lamed/L*

loʾ *heʾeminu malkhei-ʾeretz*
  vkol yosh^evei tevel
ki yavoʾ tzar v^eʾoyev
  b^eshaʿarei y^erushalai

THE FOURTH LAMENT

Long had the kings of the earth believed not,
  nor those who dwell in the world,
that enemy or foe could break
  into the gates of Jerusalem.

13. *Mem/M*

***meḥatto't** nᵉvi'eha
 'avonot kohaneha
 hashshofᵉkhim bᵉqirbah
 dam tzaddiqim*

Many were the sins of her prophets,
  profound the wickedness of her priests,
who shed righteous blood
  shamelessly in her midst -

14. *Nun/N*

***na'u** 'ivrim baḥutzot
 nᵉgo'alu baddam
 bᵉlo' yukhᵉlu yiggᵉ'u
 bilvusheihem*

Not seeing their way,
  they stumbled through her streets;
    they became soiled with blood.
So then none were able
  to touch their garments,
    soaked in impurity.

LAMENTATIONS

15. *Samek/O*

suru *tame' qar^e'u lamo*
  suru suru 'al-tigga'u
ki natzu gam-na'u 'am^{e}ru baggoyim
  lo' yosifu lagur

Outcries they make against them,
  "Away!" they call,
    "Away! Away! No closer!"
For they are exiles and wanderers,
  and those among the foreigners say,
    "Not long will they survive among us."

16. *Pe/P*

p^{e}nei *yhwh hill^{e}qam*
  lo' yosif l^{e}habbitam
p^{e}nei khohanim lo' nasa'u
  zeqeniym lo' hananu

Priests were rendered no honor;
  the elders were treated ruthlessly.
Powerful was the appearing of the Lord
  that rendered them not -
    to them he showed no mercy.

17. *Ayin/R*

'vdynh tikhlena 'eineinu
  'el-'ezratenu havel
b^{e}tzippiyyatenu tzippinu
  'el-goy lo' yoshia'

THE FOURTH LAMENT

Restlessly we watched in vain
 till our eyes grew weary.
From the watchtowers we watched
 for a nation that would save us not.

18. *Tsade/S*

tzadu *tzeʿadeinu*
 millekhet birḥovoteinu
qarav qitztzeinu maleʾu yameinu
 ki-vaʾ qitztzeinu

Stalking our steps the enemy crept –
 about our own streets we could not go.
Our end drew near –
 our days were complete,
  for our reckoning had come.

19. *Qof/T*

qallim *hayu rodefeinu*
 minnishrei shamayim
ʿal-heharim delaqunu
 bammidbar ʾarevu lanu

Terrifying were our hunters,
 swifter than the birds of prey
  soaring in the heavens.
They ran us down
 upon the mountainsides.
In ambush within the wilderness
 they crouched to pounce upon us.

20. **Resh/U**

ruaḥ *ʾappeinu mᵉshiaḥ yhwh*
  nilkad bishḥitotam
ʾasher ʾamarnu bᵉtzillo
  niḥye vaggoyim

"**Under** the shadow of the Lord's Anointed
  we shall live, though among the foreigners."
So we said, but he was captured,
  caught in the pit of the foe,
    though he was our very life's breath.

21. **Sin, Shin/V**

sisi *vᵉsimḥi bat-ʾedom*
  yoshevety bᵉʾeretz ʿutz
gam-ʿalayikh taʿavar-kos
  tishkᵉri vᵉtitʿari

Vaunt and exult yourself, O Daughter of Edom,
  you who dwells in the land of Uz.
But know this, to you also this cup will pass,
  and you will become drunk
    and strip yourself naked.

22. **Taw/W**

tam-ʿavonekh *bat-tziyyon*
  loʾ yosif lᵉhaglotekh
paqad ʾavonekh bat-ʾedom
  gilla ʿal-ḥattoʾtayikh

THE FOURTH LAMENT

Your anarchy is ended, O Daughter of Zion,
 he will no longer force you into captivity.
But your sins, Daughter of Edom, he will punish -
 he will search them out.

NOTES

One must imagine the fourth lament as a reflection on the contrast between Jerusalem prior to the siege and afterwards, between the tranquility of peace and the horror of what the war wrought. The sheer addition of cruel realities pile up on one another here. In tone and mood, it is a less personal and passionate poem than those prior to it, but it expresses all too well the completeness of the disaster that befell Zion.

Gimel-set

This is one of the only times in the entirety of this interpretation that I have simply added a verset in English —"abandoning her offspring." It carries the momentum of the line well enough, and helps a modern audience understand its meaning, unaware perhaps of either real ostrich behavior or ancient suppositions about them. As it is, ostriches do not abandon nor neglect their chicks, yet this proverbial assumption about ostriches must have been common enough for the poet to presume knowledge on the part of his audience. Note that the sense here is that Zion cannot provide sustenance and life to the children within her walls, not by ill-intent though, which makes this metaphor almost inappropriate. But it succeeds because it is hyperbolic or overstated. The totality of the suffering inside Jerusalem can only be expressed through metaphors that involve malicious harm, even when applied to the actions of Zion herself and not just the action of her besiegers. It is not irrelevant to note that caregivers do tend to feel guilt for the neglect of those they love, even if that neglect is unavoidable because of some awful present circumstance.

He-set

In *he-set*, both lines begin with the same consonant, even though this lament does return to the pattern of the first and second and does not require this alliteration at the head of each line, as in the third.

Waw-set

The sense of *waw-set* seems to be this: Judah's sin is greater than Sodom's sin, and so Judah was punished by the drawn-out agony of the Babylonian siege, whereas Sodom's "got off easy" by being destroyed in a moment by plunging right into a swift and fiery end. So the contrast lies in the duration of the punishment, and so in the amount of total pain inflicted. I rendered the order of the lines differently but conserved the original thrust.

Teth-set – Yod-set

This contrast here, in both the Hebrew and in the interpretation, echoes *waw-set*. The poet in this lament is consumed by just how slow the agonies are in a siege, how it slowly ruins and breaks everything down, turning the once compassionate and lively into desperate demons at death's door. *Yod-set*, immediately following *teth-set* here, follows this thread down its horrific length, using the image of mothers who once cared for their babies now eating them.

Lamed-set

Lamed-set begins the second half of the fourth lament, and it contains two primary themes. The first concerns the cause of the miseries, which is Judah's sin, and especially the sins of her leaders. The second is the relationship between Judah and her neighbors, the other nations that surround her. This second theme is sounded first here in this set.

Mem-set

Read Jer 11–12, 20, 26–28, 36–38. These chapters give some autobiographical context for the kind of treatment visited on an honest prophet. Within the narrative of the book of Kings, one of course finds other examples of the mistreatment of prophets leading up to the fall of Israel and then of Judah. Jeremiah's experience, though, occurred possibly within living memory of the writing of Laments and so has a relevancy to understanding the atmosphere in which such prophecies were announced and received. The irony to note is that those who were warning Judah of her impending doom were doomed themselves for doing so, persecution which only reinforced the fate reckoned upon the persecutors, according to the prophetic perspective.

Nun-set

The verset "soaked in impurity" is not in the original. I have added it, for more poetic and explanatory reasons than anything else, and I don't even have the LXX as cover in this case, I admit.

Samek-set

The effect created by *suru* and *qar^e'u* rhyming in the first verset, and then *suru suru* and *'al-tigga'u* in the second verset, all within the first line, is a little poetic detail to relish. You'll notice the same rhyme occur numerous times as well in the second line, in both versets. Just because the topic is heavy and dark doesn't mean one can't take pleasure in noticing these phonetic plays.

Pe-set

As with *he-set* before, *pe-set* also begins both lines with the same consonant.

Ayin-set

The nation in question that would "save us not" is probably Egypt. In the game of great power politics, Judah goes against the Egyptians when they should have gone for them, and for them when they should have remained loyal to Babylon (c.f. Josiah's disastrous battle with Neco II, 2 Kgs 23:28–30, and 2 Chr 35:20–27, and then compare that decision with the later desire to ally with Egypt against Babylon, read Jer 37, and, for further and rather interesting reading, go to Josephus' *Antiquities*, book 10, chapters 5–8). When Josiah attacked the Pharoah, Neco does take the opportunity to take Judah on as a kind of vassal in his war against Babylon. No doubt, this only put the kingdom of Judah all the more in the crosshairs of the Babylonians. Now they were unwillingly under the influence the Egyptians, Babylon's enemy, and thus were also demonstrated to be weak, ripe for plucking. Until then, for over a century, Judah had managed to maintain independence after the northern kingdom of Israel had succumbed to the Assyrian conquests. But with the end of Josiah's reign, over the next two decades, all this was to shift into the chaos and disaster that Laments concerns.

In the entirety of Laments, this is probably the only set that really hints at the geopolitical nature of Judah's circumstance. For the rest of the poems, the reflection has always been about the meaning of the suffering they endured in relation to God and his covenant with Israel; it is a piece of theological and ritual craftsmanship. Oddly enough, what imprecations there are against their enemies is directed towards the neighbors of Jerusalem, rather than the Babylonians themselves. The psychological reason for this may be that Babylon was a distant empire, the current occupier of what had been Assyria's role as the hammer of the Levant; it was assumed at the start that she was cruel and dangerous. But Judah's neighbors had been close to her, and the fact that some of them would have assisted a distant empire in conquering their local political cousins, so to say, must have been especially galling. The blade of someone near to you is always the hardest to see before it's used, and the sting of that kind of betrayal will always evoke the most intense desires for retribution (although, c.f. Ps 137 or Jer 50–51, Judahite literature didn't exactly lack for strong feelings about Babylon).

Resh-set

This refers to the fate of Judah's king, and, by proxy, of the line of David as a whole. For the grisly fate of Zedekiah, read 2 Kgs 25:1–7. If some hope is hinted at here for enough political independence under Babylonian rule so as to have a king still, then that surely should have seemed a moot point after Zedekiah's rebellion and a year and a half of siege. Though the gist here is a grim one without any sense of a coming restoration, it would continue to be important for the exiles to believe that one day the proper Davidic kingship could be restored. The Prophets abound with passages relevant to this hope, a hope on which the entirety of Messianism in the Jewish tradition rests. The importance of the same theological theme for the Christian tradition is obvious enough.

5

THE FINAL LAMENT

zᵉkhor yhwh me-haya lanu
  habiyta urᵉ'e 'et-ḥerpatenu
All that has befallen us, O Lord, remember.
  Look and see our ruination!

naḥalatenu nehefkha lᵉzarim
  batteinu lᵉnakhᵉrim
Both home and inheritance he passed to foreigners;
  he enriched strangers instead.

yᵉtomim hayinu 'yn 'av
  'immoteinu kᵉ'almanot
Cast out as orphans,
  we had no father -
    our mothers were as widows.

meimeinu bᵉkhesef shatinu
  'etzeinu bimḥir yavo'u

LAMENTATIONS

Doomed to haggle for our own water;
  made to buy our very own wood.

'al tzavva'renu nirdaf^e*nu*
  yaga'nu l' hunaḥ lanu
Exhausted with toil, we found no rest -
  our pursuers were at our necks.

mitzrayim natannu yad
  'ashshur lisboa' laḥem
First we begged an Egyptian,
  then an Assyrian, for bread,
    just a little to end the pangs.

'avoteinu ḥat^e*'u 'ynm*
  'nḥnv 'avonoteihem saval^e*nu*
Greatly our fathers have sinned
  and now are dead,
    but we have borne their wrongdoings.

'avadim mash^e*lu vanu*
  poreq 'ein miyyadam
Hard rule by slaves we endured,
  with none to deliver from their hand.

b^e*nafshenu navi' laḥmenu*
  mipp^e*nei ḥerev hammidbar*
It was by the risk of death we got our bread,
  for the sword of the desert is sharp.

'orenu k^e*tannur nikhmaru*
  mipp^e*nei zal'afot ra'av*
Just like an oven is heated

THE FINAL LAMENT

so our skin became hot
  with the scorching flame of famine.

nashim b^etziyyon 'innu
  b^etulot b^{e'}arei y^ehuda
Killers raped the women in Zion,
  virgins in the villages of Judah.

sarim b^eyadam nitlu
  p^enei z^eqenim lo' nehdaru
Lashed to stakes were the rulers,
  hung up by their hands.
    No honor was shown to the elders.

baḥurim t^eḥon nasa'u
  un^{e'}arim ba'etz kashalu
Men were forced to grind grain,
  boys to stagger under wood-loads.

z^eqenim mishsha'ar shavatu
  baḥurim minn^eginatam
No more are the elders in the courtyard.
  No more the youth in song.

shavat m^esos libbenu
  nehpakh l^{e'}evel m^eḥolenu
Our hearts joy has ceased from -
  to mourning turned our dancing.

naf^ela 'ateret ro'shenu
  'oy-na' lanu ki ḥata'nu
Proud was the crown toppled from our head.
  Woe to us! For we have sinned!

LAMENTATIONS

'al-ze haya dave libbenu
 'al-'elle hash^ekhu 'eineinu
So our hearts have become faint;
 so our eyes have grown dim,

'al har-tziyyon sheshshamem
 shu'alim hill^ekhu-vo
tired for the sake of Mount Zion
 where jackals now wander.

'atta yhwh l^e'olam teshev
 kis'akha l^edor vador
Unending you abide, O Lord,
 your throne generation to generation endures.

lamma lanetzaḥ tishkaḥenu
 ta'azvenu l^e'orekh yamim
Very long have you forgotten us:
 are you to abandon us forever?

hashivenu yhwh 'elekha venashuva
 ḥaddesh yameinu k^eqedem
Walk us back to you, O Lord,
 and we shall turn back:
  make our days as those before.

ki 'im-ma'os m^e'astanu
 qatzafta 'aleinu 'ad-m^e'od
Yet it seems you have forsaken us.
 With us your wrath is brimming over.

THE FINAL LAMENT

NOTES

This is the song of the children of the exiles, those who still suffered its consequences, but after the siege of Jerusalem and the scattering among the nations. It forms a proper epilogue, a dreary and mournful ending to a bitter accounting. Slowly and steadily, but sometimes with a quickened step through the horrific scenery, these laments have paced so far, dwelling upon the wasted wreck of Jerusalem and her people and all the moments of her undoing. But this poem is written as if by her children who did not see the dread and terror firsthand, but who lived with its effects, not only upon themselves but through the effect upon their parents as well.

First, the fifth lament steps down from the two lines per set that were found in the fourth and gives us just twenty-two lines, with each individual line functioning like its own set, even though the distinction between sets means basically nothing here. Really, we are looking at one set, a long stretch of twenty-two lines that stick together roughly from beginning to end. The number of lines does correspond to the same number of sets that there has been previously, that is twenty-two. But the crucial difference here is that there is no longer an acrostic structure. In its place, there is a suspiciously consistent use of rhyme within the lines, and even between them. This I think becomes the primary poetic technique, along with alliteration within the lines as well, which is also rather symmetrical in its execution. Any notion that it is a lack of skill or a loss of poetic inspiration that led to this change in form within the final lament would be mistaken. Some have thought a different poet is at work here, which may be the case, but this isn't a necessary inference. And even if it were the case that a different mind has set to crafting the last poem, again, this does not imply a definite difference in skill. There could have been a desire for a certain amount of careful asymmetry in the conclusion, so that the largest scale structure of the laments in relation to each other would not be too perfect. Perhaps this reflects the poet's, or poets', view that the state of Judah's people prior to the exile is so radically different from their state afterwards that a different kind of voice must speak at the end. As it is, the voice of the final lament is backwards looking; it is coming from the perspective of those who are already exiled or indigent in defeated Judah, and from the perspective of their children more than anyone. It is a lament of slaves and the conquered, those for whom the ancient world had little pity. To these exiles, not even God, their god, had any compassion left for them either, or so it might have seemed.

Now I decided to turn this final lament into an acrostic anyway. The only real reason for this is that my momentum was going rather in one direction by this point, and I apparently have less imagination than the original poet, so I kept to the same old trick. But I was tempted to use a rhyme scheme instead, in lieu of the consistent usage of this technique in the final lament. Most of the rhyme that is found is internal rhyme, within the lines; although there is, as pointed out already, some use of rhyming in between lines. The effect is such that in the Hebrew, there is something like the sound of couplets at points. But this rhyme occurs because of the inflected structure of Hebrew, and I was less confident of my ability to execute rhymes in English that would fit the spirit of the original source either phonetically or in emotional tone. The basic aesthetic created by English when it rhymes would not have been able, I think, to imitate the sound and feeling of

THE FINAL LAMENT

that similar effect in Hebrew. Thus, to the acrostic I held fast.

On a final technical note, the most common rhyme in the final lament comes because of the usage of both the first-person plural verbal ending -*nu*, and the first-person plural possessive suffix, which phonetically speaking is generally indistinguishable from the former. This allows the poet to attach the same phoneme to endings of both verbs and nouns thus increasing the number of situations in which he can create the rhyme. This isn't the last word on how this technique is used in this lament—there is quite a bit more to note and see—but I'll leave that to the reader.

BIBLIOGRAPHY

Alter, Robert. *The Art of Biblical Poetry*. 2nd ed. New York: Basic Books, 2011.

———. *The Hebrew Bible: A Translation with Commentary—The Writings*. Vol. 3. 3 vols. New York: Norton, 2019.

Ellinger, K., and W. Rudolph, eds. *Biblia Hebraica Stuttgartensia*. Stuttgart: Württembergische Bibelanstalt Stuttgart, 1968–76.

Brown, Francis, et al. *The Brown-Driver-Briggs Hebrew and English Lexicon*. Peabody, MA: Hendrickson, 2015.

Gesenius, Wilhelm. *Gesenius' Hebrew Grammar*. Edited by E. Kautzsch. Translated by A. E. Cowley. Mineola, NY: Dover, 2006.

The Holy Bible, Containing the Old and New Testaments with the Apocryphal/Deuterocanonical Books: New Revised Standard Version. Peabody, MA: Hendrickson, 1989.

The Holy Bible: English Standard Version, Containing the Old and New Testaments. Wheaton, IL: Crossway, 2001.

JPS Hebrew-English Tanakh: The Traditional Hebrew Text and the New JPS Translation. 2nd ed. Philadelphia: The Jewish Publication Society, 1999.

Lewis, C. S. *Reflections on the Psalms*. New York: HarperCollins, 1958.

Septuaginta: Id est Vetus Testamentum Graece iuxta LXX interpres, ed. A. Rahlfs. 8th ed. 2 vols. Stuttgart: Württembergische Bibelanstalt Stuttgart, 2006.

Slavitt, David R. *The Book of Lamentations: A Meditation and Translation*. Baltimore: Johns Hopkins University Press, 2001.

Whiston, William, trans. *The Works of Josephus*. Peabody, MA: Hendrickson, 1987.

BIBLIOGRAPHY

Ziegler, Yael. *Lamentations: Faith in a Turbulent World.* Jerusalem: Koren, 2021.

www.ingramcontent.com/pod-product-compliance
Lightning Source LLC
Chambersburg PA
CBHW061452040426
42450CB00007B/1330